Medieval Folklore

by Grace Hansen

Abdo Kids Jumbo is an Imprint of Abdo Kids
abdobooks.com

abdobooks.com

Published by Abdo Kids, a division of ABDO, P.O. Box 398166, Minneapolis, Minnesota 55439.

Abdo Kids Jumbo™ is a trademark and logo of Abdo Kids.

Printed in the United States of America, North Mankato, Minnesota.

052025

092025

Photo Credits: AdobeStock, Alamy, Everett Collection, Getty Images, Shutterstock

Production Contributors: Teddy Borth, Jennie Forsberg, Grace Hansen
Design Contributors: Candice Keimig, Pakou Moua

Library of Congress Control Number: 2024947611

Publisher's Cataloging-in-Publication Data

Names: Hansen, Grace, author.

Title: Medieval folklore / by Grace Hansen

Description: Minneapolis, Minnesota : Abdo Kids, 2026 | Series: The Middle Ages | Includes online resources and index.

Identifiers: ISBN 9798384905301 (lib. bdg.) | ISBN 9798384906001 (ebook) | ISBN 9798384906353 (Read-to-me ebook)

Subjects: LCSH: Folklore--Juvenile literature. | Cultural sociology--Juvenile literature. | Middle Ages--Juvenile literature. | Medieval history--Juvenile literature. | Dark Ages--Juvenile literature.

Classification: DDC 940.1--dc23

Table of Contents

The Middle Ages

The Middle Ages, or medieval period, was a time in European history. It lasted from about 500 to 1500 CE. Many great characters and tales of **folklore** come from this time.

Europe
Asia
Africa

Medieval Heroes

Robin Hood is a **legendary** hero. Stories about him date back as early as the 1300s. They often focus on the difficulties of life in the Middle Ages.

Robin Hood is a talented **archer**. He is best known for stealing from the rich and giving to the poor.

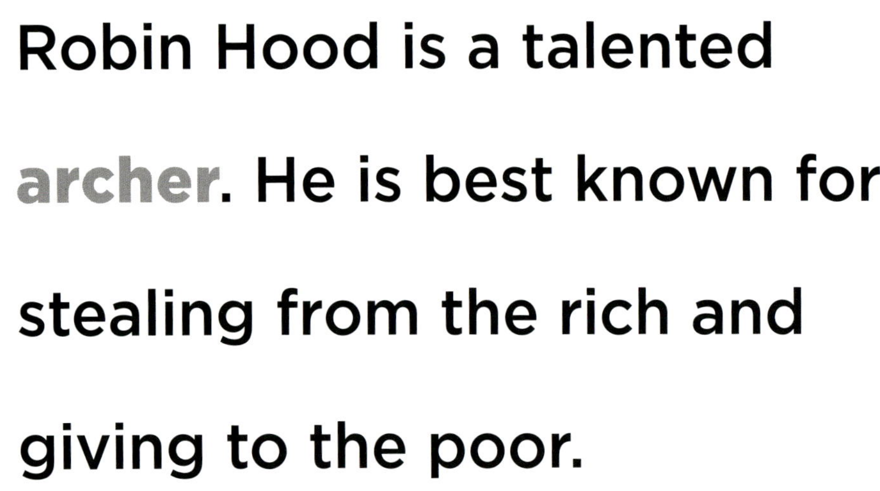

entures of
BIN HOOD

King Arthur is a **legendary** defender and ruler of Britain. Stories about him became popular in the 11th century. He may have been based on a real person or many people.

Arthur

In the earliest stories, King Arthur bravely led British forces into battle. Grander tales were later told, including *The Sword in the Stone*. In this story, a young Arthur pulls **Excalibur** from a stone where it had been magically stuck.

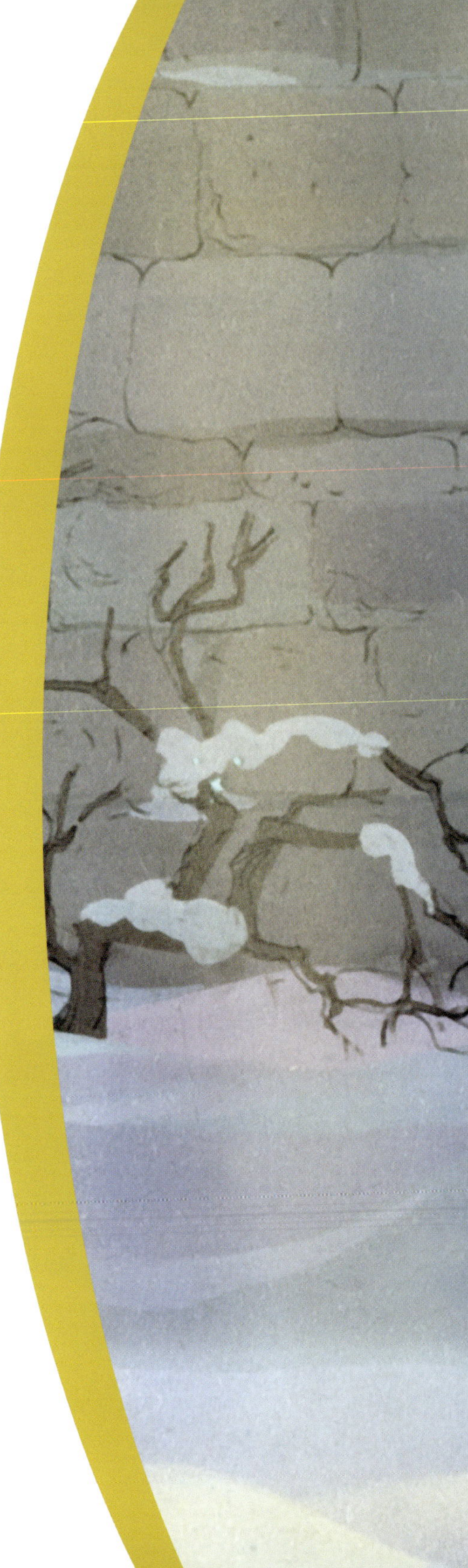

The Knights of the Round Table are also part of Arthurian legend. The Knights are tasked with keeping peace in Arthur's kingdom. Some even go on a **quest** to find a treasure called the Holy Grail.

Medieval Creatures

In medieval Europe, unicorns were described as beautiful woodland creatures. They were strong, wild, and hard to capture. Their horns could heal sickness.

In European **lore**, dragons are fire-breathing, winged monsters. They are deadly and evil. They often live in caves and guard treasures.

Dragons are covered in scales. They have a spiky tail and soar across the sky. Only the bravest heroes can defeat them.

Medieval Folklore Across Cultures

Robin Hood | **Ishikawa Goemon**

Japan

- Trained to be a ninja.
- Steals from the rich and gives to the poor.
- A popular character in Japanese theater, manga, and anime.

King Arthur | **King Vikramaditya**

India

- An ideal king who is brave, wise, and just.
- Has a group of heroes called the Nine Gems.
- Defends his kingdom from attackers.
- Sometimes uses magic.

Unicorn | **Qilin**

China

- A creature with dragon- and deer-like features.
- Shown with one horn or two horns.
- A symbol of good luck.

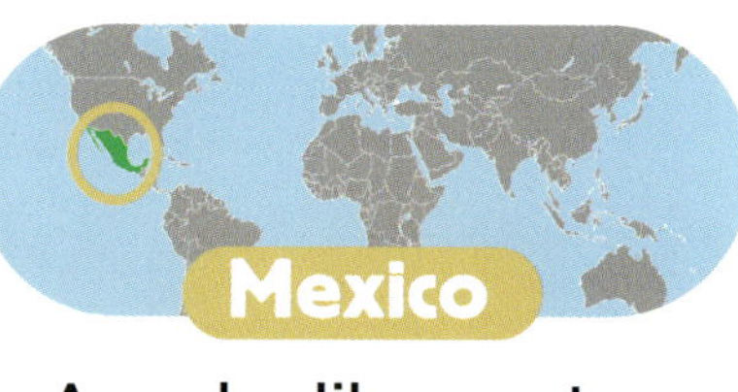

Dragon | **Quetzalcoatl**

Mexico

- A snake-like creature with feathers.
- A sign of power and wisdom.
- A god of wind and rain.
- Can be good or evil.

Glossary

archer – a person who uses a bow and arrow.

Excalibur – the sword of King Arthur.

folklore – customs, beliefs, stories, and sayings of a people handed down from generation to generation.

legendary – having to do with or like a legend. A legend is a story or group of stories that have been handed down from a time long ago and that may or may not be true.

lore – traditional knowledge or stories about a subject.

quest – a search or pursuit.

Index

Visit **abdokids.com** to access crafts, games, videos, and more!